Very Rare
GLASSWARE
of the Depression Years

Very Rare
GLASSWARE
of the Depression Years

Gene Florence

COLLECTOR BOOKS
A Division of Schroeder Publishing Co., Inc.

The current values in this book should be used only as a guide. They are not intended to set prices, which vary from one section of the country to another. Auction prices as well as dealer prices vary greatly and are affected by condition as well as demand. Neither the Author nor the Publisher assumes responsibility for any losses that might be incurred as a result of consulting this guide.

FOREWORD

First of all, I owe someone out there, a fan, the credit for the idea of an entire book devoted to rarely seen items. Nearly fifteen years ago, a man approached me at a Depression Glass Show, just after my second book had come out, saying he wished I'd make a book of only the rare items, one with big pictures of each item, so he could recognize them when he saw them. "I forget what's rare and what's common when the glass is all pictured together; but if I had a separate book to just study rarities, I could remember them real easy!" he explained. I mention the conversation later to my publisher and he filed the idea away for future consideration should the interest in Depression Glass be lasting. Well, years later with Depression Glass clubs and shows nationwide, new collectors daily discovering the excitement and fun of glassware collecting, not to mention the dollar volume generated directly and indirectly via Depression Glass, it seemed safe to assume this wasn't a short lived interest. So, nearly five years ago, the book on rarities alone was given a green light.

Rare is a relative term that has long been overused in the antiques market and in particular in describing glassware. Rarity, as defined by me in this book, is determined by lack of availability in the marketplace. Many items pictured are one-of-a-kind items or at least only one has been seen lately. Numerous patterns that are highly collectible have pieces that have never been seen by the average collector. Unique colors that were probably experimental make up a large portion of the collectibles market.

To my knowledge there has never been a book like this which tried to gather all these rarely seen items together in one frame of reference. The biggest problem would be the actual gathering, or so I thought. Convincing collectors to lend me their unique and precious glass would be difficult enough, but entrusting it to the mail or to someone else would take even more confidence. Thankfully, I was able to personally pick up much of the glassware or make arrangements for the owners to deliver it to be photographed. After months of planning the photography, a entire, hectic week was spent at two different studios in Paducah, Kentucky, and Evansville, Indiana. Photographing and re-photographing, as well as traveling to return glass and to re-borrow items that had already been returned (whose pictures failed to pass our strict standards), took up three extra weeks. (I had been naive enough to think that all my troubles were over when I got the glass together!) I had estimated on driving about 1,500 miles to accomplish this task; it was closer to 6,500 by the time all this was done.

The glassware shown in this book only encompasses the time period and patterns shown in my other Depression Era books. There is rare glass available from patterns not shown in these books, but I had to set some parameters for choosing items for the book. Various pieces seen here have never been shown in color before, and many of those that have been shown were only in my books.

I did find out that there is enough rarely seen glassware available to do this again, should you care for the concept. I will say, it will be a while before I attempt this involved process again. I originally thought it would be easier to compile this book than some of my others. However, in many ways, the strain and stress of handling other collectors' glassware was more difficult than handling my own.

Hopefully, you will appreciate all of our efforts in putting together this book on rare Depression Era glassware. I sincerely hope it helps *you* find some rare glass!

ACKNOWLEDGMENTS

I have acknowledged my debt to a fan for the original idea for this book, but the encouragement to write the book has to go to my publisher, Bill Schroeder. He mentioned actually doing this book about five years ago and it took me three years to get it started after that. From that original idea, to the fleshing out of the concept during the photography session for another book until now, the format has changed very little. It was the actual doing that was a major problem. A special thanks to Bill and to Steve Quertermous of Collector Books who worked through many sessions of photography to get the pictures as right as we could make them.

Many collectors have loaned their rare glass for you to see and each is acknowledged separately in the book. Others went beyond the call of duty to help; a special appreciation is in order for them. Beverly Hines and her friend Wanda Farque travelled from Louisiana to bring glassware to be photographed. Dick and Pat Spencer, Virgil and Joyce Krug came from Illinois; Lottie and Bill Porter came from Michigan and Jack Bell flew in from Texas, all to bring their glass for you to be able enjoy. These folks are some of the nicest and friendliest that you will ever meet. All are collectors who wish to share their treasures with fellow collectors even if it can only be done in a photograph.

The Cambridge Glass Club Museum and, in particular, Lynn Welker, who took time out of his busy schedule to help select and pack glassware from the museum to be shown in this book, have shown their willingness to share rarities with those of you who may never make it to the museum.

Thanks to Ronnie Marshall who let me take her rare Candlewick and keep it a lot longer than I had intended to do.

Dean and Mary Watkins furnished photographs of the Floragold comports; the rest of the photography was done by Donahue Studios in Evansville, Indiana, and by Curtis and Mays in Paducah, Kentucky. We especially thank Tom Clauser who labored beyond the call of duty to re-do photos that were not quite right.

Family needs to be acknowledged, particularly my wife, Cathy, who helped coordinate one photography session while I was off at another. Driving a van-load of glass is not one of her favorite things to do, especially in the snow storm and the ten degree weather that we were caught in on our way back from photographing. We had two vans of glass; so she had no choice but to drive one! Mom, "Grannie Bear", spent months getting all the glass ready for this week of photography. (I should have mentioned that we worked on pictures for two other books at the same time as this book. Somewhere, back in time, that had seemed like a good idea. Today, that seems DUMB!) The rest of the family, Chad, Marc and my Dad spent a lot of time loading and carrying this glass for me since I had a few asthma problems at the time. They, along with Charles, Sib and 'Ree, kept the home fires going while we were on the road.

Thanks to all of you! I could not and would not have done this without YOU!

Index

COVER STORY

The history of a piece of glass is hard to trace since it tells no tales as to where it's been between the manufacturing process and present ownership. Too, since there's a "profit" made from sale to sale, sellers are sometimes reluctant to divulge information regarding where, or from whom, they purchased the piece; or they simply don't know that information. When asked, they'll say "I bought it, or sold it to, some guy in a red jacket." Thus, it's rather unusual to know much "history" of a piece of glass. The wonderfully rare Mayfair shaker shown on the cover is an exception, however, and I thought you might be as intrigued as I by its colorful story in as far as I was able to trace it.

I should tell you that in early 1970, another writer had reported having seen a "different style" Mayfair shaker in the glass morgue at the factory. I was hoping to see that shaker on my visit to the Hocking factory in 1972. Unfortunately, the morgue was closed and the glass was all packed due to remodeling taking place. I had to content myself with knowing a "different style" shaker had been made by the factory and should be "out there somewhere" awaiting discovery.

In October of 1975, I had a conflict of interests. I was scheduled to attend the Michigan Depression Glass Society's show in Livonia, Michigan, but it meant missing "Court Day" in Mount Sterling, Kentucky. Although the show was an outstanding one, I hated missing that market because I'd been able to buy some good glass there in the past. So, when I flew back to Lexington on Sunday night, I called a friend who had gone to the flea market over the weekend. She told me a footed Sharon shaker had sold for $125.00. I missed teaching the next day to trace it down!

It was an unbelievable day of glass buying! The shaker had sold to another dealer along with a 15 ounce footed iced tea in Cameo! I was able to purchase both, but the shaker WASN'T Sharon; it was the Mayfair pattern; and yes, it was footed!

I then traced down the dealer who had originally owned the shaker and found out he had gotten it (with some other goodies that set me back a month's pay) at an auction near Cincinnati, Ohio.

I carried the shaker to shows from coast to coast until December of 1981 when I received a call from a collector in California who wished to purchase the round cup I had in Mayfair. He wanted something really unique for his wife for Christmas. I told him the cup was promised to someone else; so he asked me about the Mayfair shaker. I told him that several people wanted the shaker, but no one had wanted it badly enough to make me consider parting with it. He did! He wired the money to my bank and I sent it by express mail that day hoping his wife would be as happy with the shaker as mine was over the sale!

Jack Bell, another collector, started collecting pink Mayfair in June, 1984, determined to put together a complete set. To be truly "complete", he had to have the shaker. Unfortunately, I'd given my word to the buyer not to tell anyone who bought it. So, since I would only tell Jack that the shaker was sent to a buyer in California in December, 1981, he had to proceed from that scanty information to trace it down.

I asked Jack to tell you that part of the story. Here are his words:

I began to call all of the dealers in the *Daze* (Depression Glass newspaper) and even dealers who were mentioned (in the articles and Gene's book). In September 1984, I finally got the name of the Californian who had received the shaker. I started calling California information to locate the individual. The problem was this individual had an unlisted number.

I heard the individual was a Baptist Minister, so I contacted the Southwestern Theological Seminary in Fort Worth for a directory of Baptist Ministers in California. The name did not appear.

I heard the individual had a garbage collection company, so I contacted the National Refuse Association to see if the individual was a member, but to no avail.

I heard the individual was in real estate, so I had a title company run all the records for Orange county from 1982 to present, but the name did not show up.

Finally, in November 1984, I talked with an antique dealer in Orange county who knew of the individual I was trying to locate; but he had left the area. This dealer remembered that the man's children had gone to a private school down the road from his house and he gave me the name of the school. I contacted the school and got a forwarding address to Dallas, Texas—less than forty miles from my house.

I called Dallas information, but, you guessed it, the number was unlisted. I called a friend who works in Dallas and the address was less than five miles from his office. On November 22, 1984, he went to the house and made contact with the owners of the salt shaker.

At first the owners would not even talk much about the shaker, especially about selling it; but they did agree to let me see it on December 29, 1984.

In February, 1985, I met the Californian at the Houston Depression Glass show, and he told me that his wife would have to go before the shaker could be sold.

It wasn't until June, 1985 that there was any discussion about selling the shaker; and two days later, it was mine.

I think a collector as determined as that deserves to own it, don't you? I also think a shaker as rare as this one deserves a "history" as unique as the one related here!

AKRO AGATE COMPANY 1911-1951

Akro Agate Company was originally established in Akron, Ohio, in 1911. It made marbles and games there until the company moved to Clarksburg, West Virginia, in October of 1914 for economic reasons. Clarksburg offered a good grade of sand and cheap natural gas. These were the two most needed materials for making glass marbles.

World War I helped to establish Akro Agate Company as a major force in the making of marbles. Up until that war, the importing of marbles from Germany had kept Akro Agate a fledgling business. With the demise of European competition due to the war, Akro Agate was able to entrench itself in the field of marble making to the point that by the Depression years, they manufactured seventy-five per cent of the marbles made in the United States.

A competitor, Master Marbles, cut into Akro's business when it hired some of the machine designers working at Akro. For today's collectors, that was a fortuitous turning point. Because of losing business in the marble industry, Akro then turned to making other objects out of the same materials. Flower pots, planters and other utility items made by Akro grew out of the failing marble production. After obtaining the moulds from Westite Glass Company in 1936, when that factory burned, Akro issued a strong line of these items that prospered until World War II. During the last half of the 1930's, they made a line of children's doll dishes, tobacco accessory items (ash trays, match holders, etc.) and other utilitarian lines using the same glass material as had been used in their marbles. The doll or "play" dishes became a major line when "metal" play dishes disappeared due to the metals being needed for war materials. As Akro Agate had prospered during WWI, it again prospered because of WWII.

Ironically, the fate of this little company was sealed at the end of the war, however, with the introduction of plastic doll dishes which were increasingly available from Japan. In 1951, Akro was sold to Clarksburg Glass Company; and today, collectors search for that elusive trademark (crow flying through the letter A). The Akro was a shortened form of this—"as a crow".

Author's collection

COCA-COLA™ ash tray - rare embossed item

The amber "Coca-Cola™" ash tray shown in the photo was made in 1938. I have been told it may have been a souvenir item for a Clarksburg bottler. There have been numerous advertising items made into this 4″ rectangular ash tray; this, however, remains the only known Akro Agate ash tray of this type to be embossed "Coca-Cola™". It was purchased from a Clarksburg collector in 1976.

CAMBRIDGE GLASS COMPANY 1902-1958

The Cambridge Glass Company was started in Cambridge, Ohio, in 1902. Glass was made there until 1958 except for a short period in 1954-1955 when the plant was closed. Today, there is a National Cambridge Collector's Club. Many of the pieces shown in this section were borrowed from the Cambridge Museum which is operated by that club and located on Rt. 40E in Cambridge, Ohio.

The glass photographed in this section represent patterns made during a time period (1930's to 1950's) that are most collected today. Collectors of Cambridge glass began collecting the glass by colors and decorations that were distinctly Cambridge. However, as more and more Depression glass collectors started to notice the finer handmade glassware from Cambridge, dinnerware lines and sets began to be gathered. Thus, a new standard of collecting was created and the prices starting rising.

All of the glass shown in this section which was lent by Lynn Welker or Phyllis and Bill Smith can be viewed at the Cambridge Museum.

(If you are interested in joining the National Cambridge Collectors Club, their address is: National Cambridge Collectors, Inc., P.O. Box 416GF, Cambridge, Ohio 43725. Dues: $13.00 yr.)

The following pages show some of the rarest pieces of Cambridge known in the dinnerware lines with emphasis on color rarities as well as unusual pieces.

APPLE BLOSSOM amber cup and saucer - rare shape and color   From the collection of Lynn Welker

The amber square cup and saucer is line #3400/50; and the cup is referred to as four-toed. Both the cup and the color are rare in this pattern.

APPLE BLOSSOM green sugar shaker - rare item

From the collection of Lynn Welker

The light emerald green sugar shaker is rare enough that it has never been shown in any book in color. All sugar shakers in etched Cambridge patterns are hard to find. So, watch for them!

APPLE BLOSSOM amethyst plate with silver decoration - rare color

From the collection of Lynn Welker

The amethyst, silver decorated plate gave two photographers headaches! Either the design would show black instead of silver or the plate would not show its true color! For those who have tried to photograph glass, you do understand how difficult glassware can be to capture on film. I hope you will appreciate the effort and expense to give you quality photographs!

CAPRICE crystal punch bowl and candle reflectors - rare items

Although the Caprice punch bowl was made in Cambridge's latter years, thus far only a few have surfaced. This crystal Caprice punch bowl was purchased from a lady of Australian heritage at the Georgetown Antique Mall (Ky) in December of 1984. Although it was damaged, it made an interesting addition to the Caprice display at the Cambridge Musuem. The candle reflectors shown were found in Michigan.

CAPRICE blue candlestick - rare item and color

    The Moonlight blue Caprice #69 7½″ 2-lite candlestick with candle cups shaped like seashells is wanted by many Caprice collectors. Occasionally, one is found in crystal, but rarely in blue.

CAPRICE red candlestick - rare color

From the collection of Lynn Welker

   This Carmen Caprice #1338 6″ 3-lite candlestick only surfaced recently. What other Carmen rarities are awaiting discovery?

CAPRICE amethyst goblet and mulberry cup and saucer - rare colors

This amethyst goblet turned up at the National Cambridge Antique show in 1986.

CLEO green temple jar - rare item

From the collection of Georgeann Henry

The green Cleo temple jar was purchased in a California shop several years ago. Two of the collectors who have lent glass for this book were in the shop together, but only one was lucky enough to become the proud owner. It does prove that good glass can be found in the Western United States.

DIANE amethyst silver decorated bowl - rare color

The amethyst silver decorated #3400 Diane 12″ bowl came from California. The owner was willing to ship it for use in this book. The silver overlay certainly makes the pattern stand out!

DIANE Heatherbloom cigarette box - rare color

Diane pattern in Heatherbloom color is quite unusual; and even though the #1312 footed cigarette box was found after two major photography sessions, special arrangements were made for it to be included here. Enjoy!

Author's collection

DIANE Heatherbloom perfume and Crown Tuscan card holder - rare colors

The #3400 two-ounce perfume in Heatherbloom, like all etched patterns in this color, remains elusive. The #1066 gold-encrusted Crown Tuscan oval cigarette or card holder is hard to find.

DIANE pink dinner plate - rare color

I will bet that you have not seen this #3400 Peach-blo dinner plate very often!

ELAINE amethyst gold-encrusted bud vase - rare color

The #274 10″ bud vase in gold-encrusted Elaine on amethyst is quite a find. As usual the gold on this vase really thrusts the design to the forefront. Encrusted items were meant to be special, and they are!

From the collection of Lynn Welker

GLORIA yellow decanter - rare item

The Gold Krystol #1322 26-ounce Gloria decanter would add to any collection of Gloria—if you could find one!

From the collection of Bill & Phyllis Smith

GLORIA yellow with amber foot goblet - rare item and color

The #3025 ten-ounce goblet with amber stem and foot is even more unusual than the decanter; but it would drive you to the brink of insanity trying to find other goblets to go with it! We're just grateful to see this one.

From the collection of Lynn Welker

HUNT SCENE amber gold-encrusted decanter - rare item

The amber, gold-encrusted Hunt Scene #3075, 28 oz. handled decanter is improved by the added gold. This has been one of my wife's favorite Cambridge patterns; but being from "horse country" in Kentucky, I guess that would not be considered out of the ordinary.

From the collection of Lynn Welker

HUNT SCENE gold-encrusted Avocado goblet - rare color

From the collection of Lynn Welker

The Avocado, gold-encrusted goblet proved to be a difficult item to photograph. The thin panels had a tendency to disappear and make the goblet look damaged. The pattern certainly stands out with the gold decorations.

HUNT SCENE green footed fish bowl - rare item

For those of you who are wondering about the light Emerald footed piece, as I did when I first saw it—a fish bowl is the right answer. I wonder what color a goldfish appears in a green bowl.

Author's collection

From the collection of Lynn Welker

MOUNT VERNON Emerald mustard, Carmen candlestick, Violet sherbet - rare colors

Mount Vernon is a pattern that has a variety of colors. Indeed, the list of colors is almost as long as its variety of pieces. The opaque, purplish color was called Violet by Cambridge, and is often confused with the Helio color. The Violet shades more toward blue than Helio; but the difference is not very obvious unless the pieces are side by side—an occurrence which seldom happens.

PORTIA Heatherbloom pitcher and tumbler - rare color

Etched Heatherbloom items are all difficult to find. The #3400 pitcher came from Louisiana and the #3400 tumbler from Ohio.

PORTIA Carmen gold encrusted vase - rare color

Portia pattern is represented by this gold-encrusted Carmen #3400 5″ globe vase. When I chose the items to be shown in this book, I was delighted to find so many colored, gold-encrusted pieces—both for their scarcity and for the fact that they show the pattern designs so well in photographs!

ROSALIE or #731 Carmen wine goblet - rare color

The #3130 wine goblet was found at the Heisey Show in 1986. Many times, more than Heisey is found at that show in Newark!

ROSEPOINT amber, gold encrusted pitcher - rare color

ROSEPOINT amber, gold encrusted tumbler - rare color

From the collection of Austin & Shirley Hartsock

ROSEPOINT amber sugar - rare color

The amber #3400 sugar in Rosepoint is one of the few pieces found in that color. Rosepoint is the one pattern name that many people think of when they hear the name Cambridge. Since it is normally seen in crystal, colored pieces are doubly noticed by collectors. This amber sugar still needs to find its creamer mate. Have you seen one?

ROSEPOINT Carmen gold encrusted pitcher - rare color

The Carmen gold-encrusted ball jug is a beautiful piece of glass! In fact, my publisher thought it was the best looking piece of glass that we had at the photography session. You have to know that he prefers largemouth bass, Canadian geese and ducks over any form of glassware to appreciate what high praise that was!

ROSEPOINT Ebony, gold-encrusted vase - rare color

The Ebony, gold-encrusted vase turned out to be the most difficult piece of glass to photograph in this book. Its shiny black surface, as well as the black color itself, threw the photographers into pandemonium. Again, collectors take notice of any colored Rosepoint, a popular pattern normally seen in crystal.

MISCELLANEOUS little items - rare colors

PORTIA Gold Krystol #3400 3″ nut cup
GLORIA Light Emerald #3400 3″ nut cup
CLEO Gold Krystol #3077 cordial

From the collection of Lynn Welker

DUNCAN & MILLER GLASS COMPANY 1893-1955

The new Duncan & Miller Glass Company was incorporated in 1900. Its roots were the old Duncan Glass Company, which had begun in Pittsburgh, but was moved to Washington, Pennsylvania, in 1893. Glassware made at this factory is eagerly sought by many collectors today.

However, it is the patterns that were made during the Depression years and beyond that are the most in demand. The Caribbean pattern, introduced in 1936 and discontinued in 1955 when the factory closed, continues to attract collectors because of it's beautiful color and line.

Author's collection

CARIBBEAN blue cordial - rare piece

The 3″, one ounce cordial shown here represents one of the most difficult pieces of Caribbean to find although, considering the longevity of the line, none of this pattern is what I would call plentiful in today's antique market place.

FENTON ART GLASS COMPANY 1907 to Date

The first glass was made at this plant in 1907. Williamstown, West Virginia, has been its home since then. Fenton was known more for their making of Carnival and Art glass than for the making of Depression patterns. One major pattern with a multitude of colors does stand out. Lincoln Inn was introduced in 1928 and was made as recently as the early 1980's in a iridescent purple color.

Fenton Art Glass has become one of the few major glass companies to be able to operate in today's market. Many gift shops still carry Fenton's line and it has been their adaptability to change with the public's demand that has kept their glassware in the changing world.

From the collection of Beverly & Earl Hines

LINCOLN INN blue pitcher and tumbler - rare color and items

The 7¼″ 46-ounce pitcher has only turned up twice. Both of these were found within a three-month period and none have been spotted since. The nine-ounce flat tumbler was found with the first pitcher and no others have surfaced since then.

FOSTORIA GLASS COMPANY 1887-1986

Fostoria Glass Company almost survived a century! That included a major move from Fostoria, Ohio, to Moundsville, West Virginia, in the early days. Lancaster Colony bought Fostoria in the early 1980's; but even the glassware in the morgue at the factory was sold in December, 1986.

The American pattern, first begun in 1915, was one of the longest made patterns in the U.S. glassmaking history! Lancaster Colony will probably continue to make some pieces available in this pattern, perhaps through Indiana Glass Company.

AMERICAN amber cologne bottle - rare color

This amber cologne bottle was one of two found on an amber tray several years ago at a bargain price of $30.00. VERY little amber was made in American! It is the crystal that most people are familar with today.

From the collection of Dick & Pat Spencer

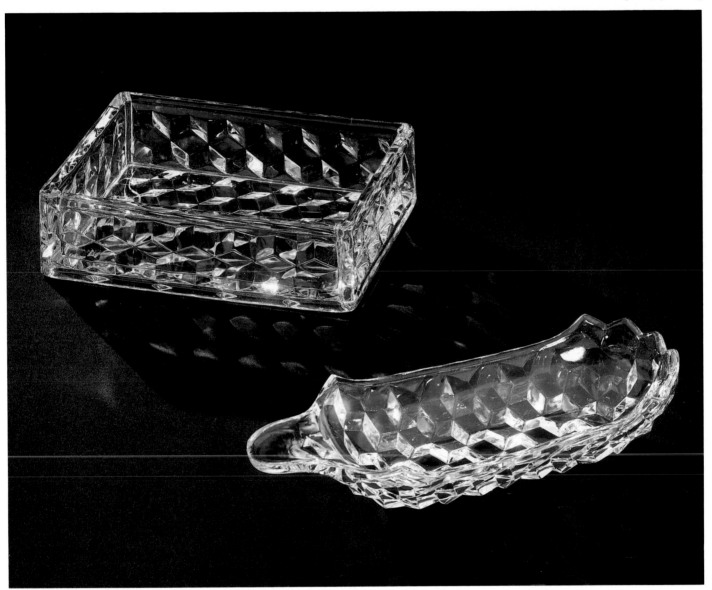

AMERICAN crystal banana split and chocolate box - rare pieces

Since so many people collect American, items in short supply seem to stay that way. Banana split dishes and this chocolate box are rarely seen. Note the chocolate box does not have a lid.

AMERICAN crystal bowl and pitcher - rare items

A wash bowl and pitcher has to be seen to be believed! These were for hotel use. With the weight of this set without water, I can imagine that maids were rather glad to see these broken and replaced with some lighter china ones.

AMERICAN crystal crushed fruit - rare item

From the collection of Virgil & Joyce Krug

A 10″ crushed fruit jar is missing from many collections of American. Originally, there was a glass 9″ crushed fruit spoon for this jar.

AMERICAN crystal handled tea, handled sherbet and soap dish - rare items

Handled iced teas and handled sherbets were surely experimental or were produced in extraordinarily small supply. Of course, these were both made earlier than many of the well-known pieces we see today. We removed the lid of the soap dish so that the raised partitions in the bottom could be seen.

From the collection of Virgil & Joyce Krug

AMERICAN crystal flower pot with perforated cover - rare item

   The flower pot has a perforated cover, and it is still one of my favorite pieces of American. It takes a lot of flowers to fill that monster. I wonder how many of these were ever actually used for that purpose.

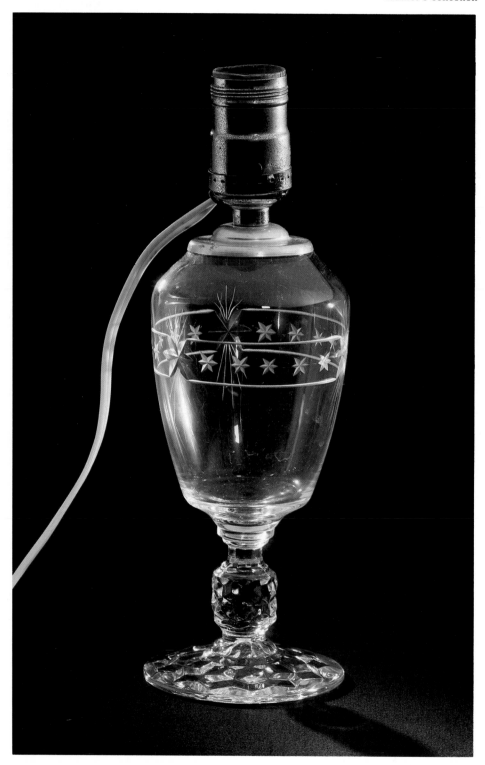

AMERICAN LADY crystal lamp - rare item

American Lady is the name given to the #5056 line of American stemware with a plain (no pattern) top. The lamp shown was probably a water goblet which was not sheared off. It was cut with a star pattern for a striking effect. This seems to be a non-production item; but it does make a rare piece of glass.

BAROQUE green candlestick - rare color

Baroque pattern in a green color is highly unusual. There seem to be very few pieces available to be collected; but isn't it beautiful?

CHINTZ crystal syrup pitcher - rare item

    To my knowledge, this Chintz crystal syrup pitcher is not listed in any catalogues! The mould is shown, however.

COLONY crystal ice bucket - rare item

Colony has become another Fostoria pattern many have suddenly rushed to find. The ice bucket shown has a collar flange around the top which is not the one normally seen. This was shown in a 1941 catalogue.

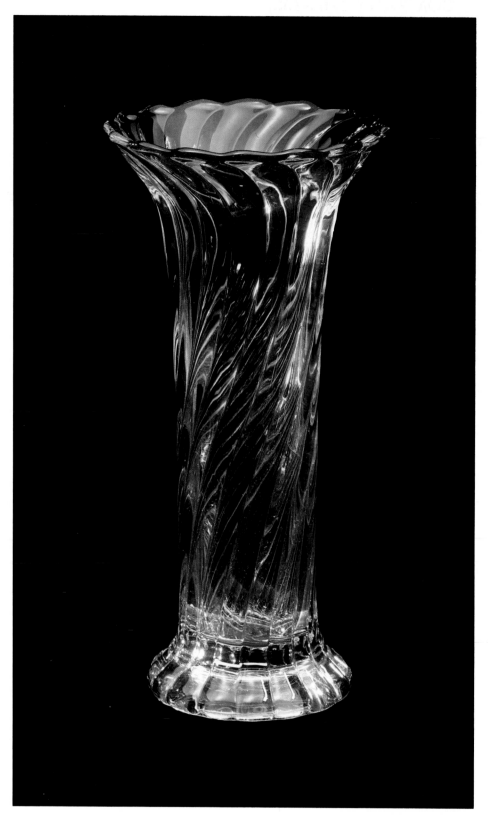

COLONY crystal vase - rare item

Author's collection

The 11″tall Colony vase is a super piece of glass that surprised me when I first saw it, as I had never seen this in any catalogue. Take note that the voices of Fostoria collectors are beginning to be heard throughout the field of collecting.

FRY GLASS COMPANY 1901-1933

Fry Glass Company manufactured cut glass when the factory started in 1901. As the demands for this glass decreased, Fry was able to switch styles (following the dictates of the American consumer) and make glass for daily use.

Fry Glass Company's opalescent color that most collectors already associate with oven ware or reamers was called Pearl Glass by the company. Fry pinks and greens, colors most often associated with the Depression era glassware, are not easily found. Ice buckets were made in pink, green and cobalt blue. Cobalt blue Fry is extremely hard to find. Lids to any colored Fry ice buckets are scarce.

From the collection of Kenn & Margaret Whitmyer

FRY cobalt ice bucket - rare color.

HAZEL-ATLAS GLASS COMPANY 1902-1956

Hazel-Atlas was formed from the merger of Hazel Glass Company and Atlas Glass and Metal Company in 1902. Production of containers and tumblers were their main concern until the Depression years. In the 1930's, starting with kitchenware items such as colored mixing bowls, they quickly branched into dinnerware patterns.

The Shirley Temple bowl, mug and creamer that are recognized by almost everyone were made by Hazel Atlas. Sets of Royal Lace and Moderntone in Ritz blue (cobalt) were advertised together for the same price: 44 pieces for $2.99! Now, there is a much greater price range in those patterns!

In recent years, it has been the kitchenware made by Hazel-Atlas that has come to the forefront. Again, the popularity of Ritz blue has pushed the prices of that color well above the prices for pink and green. Mixing bowls, measuring cups and reamers all command premium prices. The piece may be rarer in some other color, but collector demand pushes the price of the blue well beyond those of any other color.

MODERNTONE pink cup and saucer - rare color

The pink Moderntone cup and saucer may not excite many collectors who think of this pattern only in terms of blue or amethyst; but cup and saucer collectors know how truly rare this set is in pink!

A.H. HEISEY & COMPANY 1896-1957

The A.H. Heisey & Company opened its door in 1896. Their handsome pressed glassware was a success. In fact the innovative idea of advertising glassware in national publications is attributed to Heisey. Glass was made continuously at the plant site in Newark, Ohio, until 1957. As with Cambridge, the glassware made in the 1930's to 1950's is the most collectable today.

One of the most difficult problems facing new collectors comes from the fact that the Heisey moulds were bought by Imperial in 1958, and many pieces were made at that plant until its demise in 1984. New collectors have to learn the Imperial colors because some of these pieces made by Imperial are similar to rare Heisey colors. Crystal pieces are more difficult to distinguish and collectors are beginning to accept this fact. All of those Heisey/Imperial moulds were repurchased by the Heisey Collectors and are now back in Newark, Ohio. So, there should be no danger of reissues being made from these moulds again.

From the collection of Gary & Sue Clark

CRYSTOLITE crystal cake stand - rare item

The Crystolite pattern has a few pieces that are difficult to find. While many items are plentiful, it is hard to imagine how much trouble some of this Heisey line can cause an ardent collector. The cake plate shown here was purchased at a show in Eugene, Oregon, and brought back home to Newark for the Heisey show. It now resides in Missouri.

CRYSTOLITE crystal vase and goblet - rare items

The 12″ vase has only recently been discovered and the #1503 goblet has always been elusive. Normally, Crystolite is found on #5003 stemware.

GREEK KEY crystal toothpick - rare item

The Greek Key shot glass (or toothpick) shown is found in very few collections. For some unknown reason, all of the stemware in Greek Key is elusive, but the shot glass is even more so.

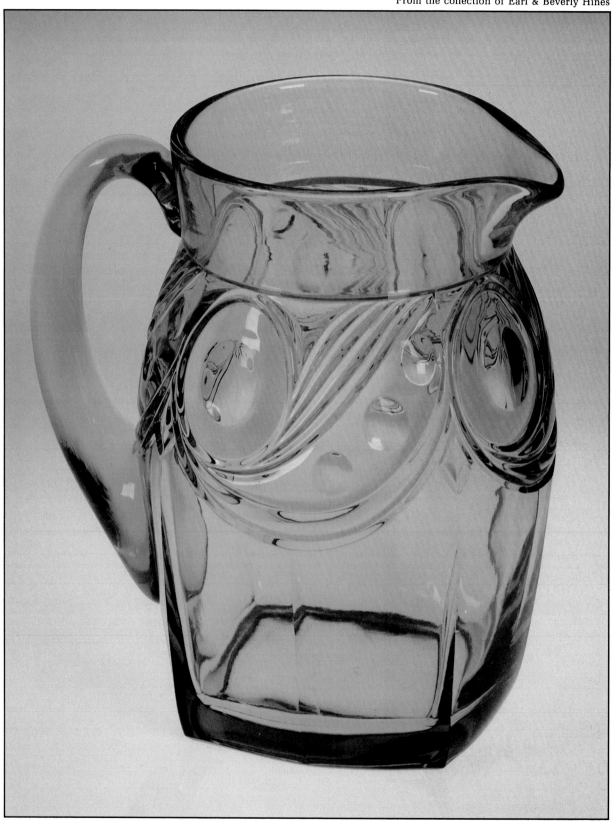

IPSWICH green pitcher - rare item

    The Ipswich pitcher in green was brought from Louisiana to be photographed. Although a collector of green Ipswich was at the photography session, he could not talk the owner into letting him take it back to Illinois with him, no matter how hard he tried. Enjoy! You will not see many of these.

LARIAT crystal black-out lights and black plate - rare items

Lariat in black has only shown up as plates and there are precious few of those. The crystal items shown on each side of the black plate are black-out lamps. Unfortunately, the shades are missing; they make the lamps 7″ high when in place. The shade is a straight, cylindrical shape, 5″ tall. This shade rests ½″ inside the lamp when placed upon the 2½″ bottom.

MINUET Crystal - Candlevase - rare item

The small vase that sits atop this piece is the most elusive part.

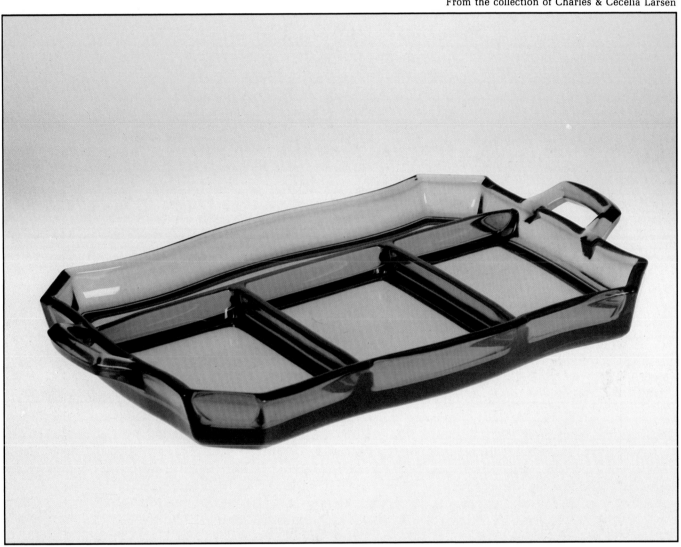

OCTAGON Dawn relish tray - rare color

Dawn is the color name of the 12″ Octagon relish. In this case, the name is apt since this tray was bought just before sunrise in 1984 at the Flea Market around the Courthouse square in Newark, Ohio. Heisey collectors are out at that market with flashlights looking for bargains; and this was a bargain at $30.00!

ROSE crystal epergnette - rare item

Author's collection

The Heisey 3-light candlestick in Rose is not the focus of the picture. The rarity is the 6″ deep epernette with the Rose etching sitting atop the candlestick. The epernette can also be found with Orchid etching. Neither are in many collections.

TWIST green cocktail shaker - rare item

The Twist cocktail shaker in Moongleam (green) was thought to be a lamp base by those who saw it before this one turned up at a show in Marietta, Georgia. There was still some skepticism about the authenticity of the piece because the top shown here did not fit well even though it had been found on the piece. When the moulds were bought from Imperial by the Heisey Club, not only was the mould found for this piece, but the original drawings as well—proving once and for all that this was a cocktail shaker. It was so rarely seen, questions were natural.

From the collection of Dick & Pat Spencer

WAVERLY amber candy - rare color

Waverly rarely turns up in any Heisey color, but the amber candy with lid is an exception to this rule. Isn't it striking?

ALEXANDRITE - rare color and item

From the collection of Dick & Pat Spencer

Alexandrite color in Heisey is a very desirable color. The #1150 Colonial Star plate was made for B. Altmans as a special order from the Newark factory in 1938. Evidently, this was only done once; today, not many of these seem to have survived. At any rate, few have surfaced.

DAWN - rare color and rare items

Dawn was one of the last Heisey colors introduced. The Lodestar candleblocks have rarely been seen before. This should give candlestick collectors another headache in their searching. Collectors of shakers and small Heisey items will also get one from searching for that rarely seen Saturn shaker.

TANGERINE - rare color (opposite page)

Tangerine is a color uniquely Heisey. There are other companies who tried similar colors, but none who came close. The favor vase is not often found, although it is one of those unmarked items that sometimes turns up at a bargain price; so be aware of that.

From the collection of Charles & Cecelia Larsen

HOCKING GLASS COMPANY 1905 to Date

Hocking became today's Anchor-Hocking in 1937, but nearly all of the glassware shown in this section was made before the year of that merger. The people who work at this factory have always helped me in every way they could in my research because they realize the historical significance of our glass. I am truly grateful.

From the collection of Bill & Lottie Porter

BUBBLE pink cup and saucer - rare color

Bubble pattern was produced in almost every color that Hocking made over the years. This is especially true of the large berry bowl. The only plentiful piece in pink is that particular bowl. A cup and saucer in pink was found years ago, but few others have surfaced.

CAMEO crystal relish - rare color

From the collection of Dan Tucker & Lorrie Kitchen

Although commonly found in green, this is one of the few seen in crystal.

CAMEO green lamp base - rare item

An uncut, 5″ tumbler was used to create this rare lamp base.

From the collection of Dan Tucker & Lorrie Kitchen

CAMEO green lamp base - rare item

A kerosene screw-on burner fits the top of this high sherbert to convert it to a lamp.

CAMEO green sandwich server - rare item

CAMEO yellow butter dish - rare color

Cameo in yellow has always been in short supply except for the ever present dinner sets that Hocking heavily promoted. Only a few butter dishes have surfaced. Some extra butter dish bottoms have turned up, but few tops. It is the bottom in the green that is hard to find. That is what is so interesting in this business. The same pieces are rarer in one color than they are in others; top parts are rare in one color, bottoms in another. Fascinating!

CAMEO yellow milk pitcher - rare item

This yellow, 20 oz., pitcher was found about ten years ago at Washington Court House, Ohio. It is the only one that has been seen to date.

COLONIAL pink beaded top pitcher - rare item

Colonial pink pitchers are rather plentiful. The pink, beaded top pitcher is not. In fact, it remains unique at this writing. It was purchased the same day as the footed Mayfair shaker in October, 1975. It remains a mystery to me why only one of this style has ever been found.

COLONIAL red footed tumbler - rare color

Author's collection

Perhaps the red Colonial tumbler was an experimental line of the 1938 Royal Ruby promotions. If it were, then it would have been made by Anchor-Hocking. However, when I took a flat water tumbler to the factory years ago, it was thought to be pre-Royal Ruby promotion. In any case, this is only the second piece of Colonial I have ever seen in red.

From the collection of Bill & Lottie Porter

FIRE-KING DINNERWARE blue cup and saucer - rare item

    Fire-King dinnerware has remained an elusive pattern of Hocking. When I was working on my first book in 1972, I saw a whole display of this pattern at the factory. During the 1970's, much of this glassware was found in the marketplace. The cup and saucer shown here were found at Washington Court House, Ohio, in 1978, along with several other pieces of blue. This is the only cup known in any color!

MAYFAIR green, pink and frosted pink console bowls - rare items

Mayfair console bowls are the dream of every collector of this pattern, but very few have been found. For a piece to be so rare, it is amazing that there are two different styles. Note that the green and the pink both have a ribbed edge whereas the frosted pink has a plain edge. The pink has been found both ways; but since the frosted pink and the green are the only console bowls known in those colors, I chose to show this style of pink.

The first console bowl to show up was brought to a Depression Glass show in Cincinnati in 1971. I later borrowed it for the cover of my first book. It had been purchased for $7.00 earlier that year. I mention that price because it is the same price that the green one was bought for in North Carolina - only thirteen years later when many more people knew about the value of this glass!

From the collection of Jack Bell

From the collection of Jack Bell

MAYFAIR pink footed shaker - rare item

From the collection of Jack Bell

The story of the footed shaker is told as the cover story of this book.

MAYFAIR pink, five-part relish - rare color

The five-part relish in pink is unusual. This piece is commonly found in crystal and sometimes in a metal tray. In pink, only this one has ever been found. Keep looking! There must be a few others!

MAYFAIR yellow butter dish and sugar with lid - rare color   From the collection of Earl & Beverly Hines

Mayfair in yellow was never listed in any of Hocking's catalogues, but there are numerous pieces to be found. There are two styles of butter bottoms. The regular butter bottom which served as a 7″ vegetable bowl and which is the same as found in pink and blue. The indented bottom with a ledge for the top to rest upon as shown here, has only been found in yellow and crystal. Strangely enough, there have been no crystal tops found. The sugar bowl in yellow is like the Cameo butter in that one piece is easier to find than the other. In this case the bottom has been found only twice while three tops have appeared. One complete sugar bowl was found in the Cincinnati area in the late 1970's when it was brought in to a Depression show there. Another lid was found in the same town at a Mall show for $5.00. The last lid to show up was bought in an Antique Shop for $3.15 three years ago. It had been found under the floor of a log cabin in Eastern Kentucky. Bargains do exist if you are in the right place at the right time. It usually works out that you have to be in many wrong places at the wrong time to get lucky enough to make it the right time once. Believe me, I know!

Author's collection

MAYFAIR yellow cookie jar - rare color

This is the first complete yellow cookie discovered. It was found after the book was finished, so provisions were made to include it.

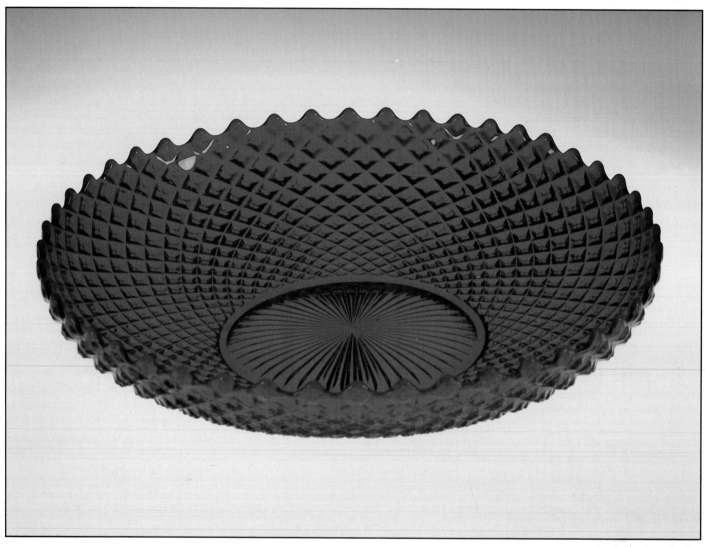

MISS AMERICA red bowl - rare item and color

Red Miss America is not often seen and then it is usually stemware or the creamer and sugar. A few bowls have turned up but none like the one shown here. This console bowl has not surfaced in any other color. It still has the original label on it although the photographer decided not to show it.

PRINCESS yellow juice pitcher - rare color

From the collection of Earl & Beverly Hines

Yellow Princess juice pitchers have been found in Kentucky in the past. In fact, two of the three known came from Falmouth and Lexington. In the early 1970's, I went to look at some glass in a home here. The lady was mixing frozen orange juice under the kitchen faucet in this pitcher. She had decided to collect yellow Princess so I was not able to buy it. A few years later when she had tired of trying to put together a set, she called to sell me her collection and I bought it all to get this pitcher.

REAMER "Mayfair" blue - rare color   From the collection of Kenn & Margaret Whitmyer

The blue, two part reamer has remained an elusive prize even after being pictured in my Kitchenware books. Surely there are more of these just waiting to be discovered by some lucky collector.

WATERFORD pink goblet and juice - rare items

Waterford in the Miss America style has confused collectors for years. The pattern is definitely Waterford; but it was made from the mould style of Miss America. Note the rings above the pattern and the shapes. These are just the way the rings occur on Miss America but not on the normal Waterford pieces. Two of the goblets were found at an auction in Southeastern Kentucky. In those days, Depression Glass did not get top billing at auctions, but this auction had a large accumulation of Depression Glass in an old barn. Two collectors from Ohio bought these goblets and each took one. The juice tumbler was bought at a Flea Market in Ohio. Are there any others out there awaiting discovery?

IMPERIAL GLASS CORPORATION 1904-1984

Although glass making began at Imperial in 1904, it was the start of a new era in 1936 when Candlewick was introduced for the first time. Until the company's demise in 1984, Imperial turned out a multitude of pieces in this one pattern, but it was not their ONLY pattern.

BEADED BLOCK white pitcher - rare color

From the collection of Mrs. Harold Workman

The Beaded Block pitchers have always been difficult to find and although the white milk glass one is shown in catalogues, I had only seen pieces of one until now. Pieces is the operative word. One of my publisher's employees had brought one to the office for me to see. His mother had just recently found it and wanted me to verify the pitcher for her. As the boy came in the door, a gust of wind caught the door and knocked it against the sack in which the pitcher was being carried. The pitcher was shattered and that is why I had only seen pieces. However, a lady in Michigan found this one at a garage sale for fifty cents and I was able to borrow it to photograph.

CANDLEWICK black, two-handled bowl - rare color

From the collection of Dick & Pat Spencer

Black Candlewick was made in a limited number of pieces. Most of these pieces were hand decorated with flowers of white, gold and red. I bought six black goblets that had been purchased at Imperial in 1976 for $3.00 each. Goblets were not decorated as most of the other black pieces were. The bowl shown here was sold for only $30.00 a few years ago.

CANDLEWICK cobalt blue sherbet - rare color   From the collection of Ronnie Marshall

The #3800 cobalt blue sherbet is one of the few pieces that I have seen in that color. I am sure that there are more somewhere. Let's find them!

CANDLEWICK crystal cut goblet - rare item

The #3800 cut goblet was bought at the factory closeout. It may have been experimental. I would like to think more are available because it is a beautiful piece of glass.

CANDLEWICK crystal bowl on stem and handled bowl - rare items

From the collection of Ronnie Marshall

The 6″ cottage cheese bowl on the four-bead stem and the 6″ handled bowl are both experimental pieces shown for the first time. Since all of the glass was sold out of the closed factory, undoubtedly more unusual pieces will be showing up as time goes by.

CANDLEWICK crystal handle vase and sherbet - rare items

From the collection of Ronnie Marshall

One of the rarest lines of Candlewick is the #195 as shown by the sherbet next to the 8½″ handled vase. The handled vase (400/227) looks more like a handled pitcher than a vase. Both of these pieces were regular production items, which means that they should be available with diligent searching.

CANDLEWICK gold inlaid on glass - rare color

From the collection of Ronnie Marshall

Probably the most desirable Candlewick item is the inlaid gold on glass punch set that was first sold in the early 1940's. It was expensive for that time—$125.00. That still holds true today! Also shown is the oval snack plate and cup with gold decoration. Fifty pieces of this gold decorated Candlewick were bought in February, 1983, for $900.00. What a bargain!

From the collection of Ronnie Marshall

CANDLEWICK green - rare color

Two pieces of green Candlewick were found in Rochester, New York, in September, 1986, for $4.50. One is the 6″ 400/3F bowl and the other is the 5¼″ 400/23B. I have not been able to find out much about this color except that several collectors are hot on its trail.

From the collection of Ronnie Marshall

CANDLEWICK red bowl - rare color

Red Candlewick was made in several pieces, and the four-toed bowl (74SC) is one of my favorites. I would love to have a cordial in that color for my collection!

CANDLEWICK red candlesticks - rare color

From the collection of Ronnie Marshall

These 400/40C candlesticks arrived after all the photography was finished, but they are so rare they had to be included.

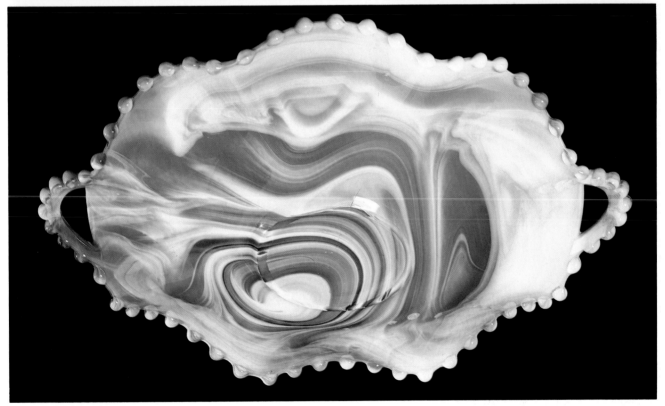

CANDLEWICK slag plate - rare color

Slag Candlewick is represented by the 12″ crimped, two-handled plate (400/145C). It is photographed on both sides to show the variations in the slag. The back has a better slag effect than the front. This piece was found for only $10.00 at a Flea Market in Ohio. See, bargains do exist. You just need to know what is rare!

As you can tell, there is more available in Candlewick than just crystal. With over six hundred moulds in the line and almost fifty years of production, the future looks bright for Imperial's Candlewick collectors.

CANDLEWICK slag plate - rare color

From the collection of Dan Tucker & Lorrie Kitchen

INDIANA GLASS COMPANY 1907 TO DATE

Indiana Glass has caused concern for collectors for years with their "re-issues". A more proper term might be reproductions! It is a shame because many pieces of their glass fit the "rare" category.

From the collection of Darlene Kouri

"DAISY", NUMBER 620 blue plate - rare color

The Daisy 9⅜" dinner plate is the only piece of blue I have ever seen. It was bought at a basement sale in Chicago for seventy-five cents.

"PYRAMID", NUMBER 610 yellow ice bucket and lid - rare item

The yellow Pyramid ice bucket turns up infrequently, but it is the lid that is the rarer part of this duo.

JEANNETTE GLASS COMPANY

Jeannette Glass Company seemed to have an affinity for making odd colored glass from their standard glassware lines. Canary yellow (vaseline), red or even transparent blue turns up in patterns once in a while. To make this fact even more astounding is that those colors were not part of their repertoire in other patterns either. It's as if they wanted to cause us wonderment years later.

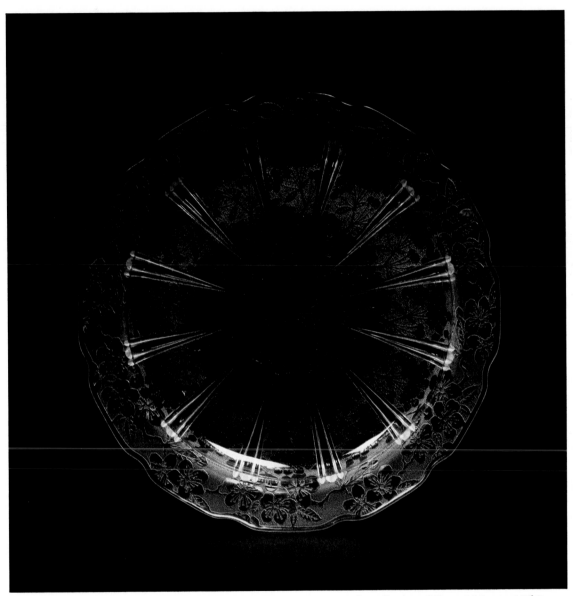

From the collection of Kenn & Margaret Whitmyer

CHERRY BLOSSOM pink plate - rare style

Note the shape of the Cherry Blossom plate and the design on it. The flanged edge is unlike the normal Cherry dinner plates. Many collectors have been shying away from Cherry Blossom because of the reproductions; but this is the genuine article. This particular plate also turned up in a transparent light blue. Since Cherry has also been found in yellow, red and even Jadite, it stands to reason that there may have been other colors tried over the years that Cherry Blossom pattern was in production. So keep a sharp eye!

Author's collection

CUBE canary yellow powder jar - rare color

The Cube footed powder jar was found in northern Ohio several years ago. There was also a blue one. This jar, the blue one and the Windsor shown later—all were found in the same house, probably indicating some connection to a worker at the factory.

Many of the odd pieces that are found today were made at lunch or after hours. "Lunch pail" glass is the title that has been given to this glass that made its way out of the factory in a lunch box as gifts to friends or family.

DORIC delphite pitcher - rare color

From the collection of Earl & Beverly Hines

The delphite Doric pitcher is the only one that has even been seen. The photographer did an excellent job in showing the glue line. Alas, it's not perfect, but still unique! The same uniqueness applies to the yellow Doric. It, along with yellow Adam cups, round saucers and plates, and yellow Cherry bowls were found in 1972. My first book had just come out and I was still teaching school. I was only able to buy the Adam cups and one of the two Cherry bowls. I did not have an extra $38.00 to buy the other bowl. All of this came out of a basement of an ex-Jeannette employee's home in western Pennsylvania.

DORIC yellow pitcher - rare color

From the collection of Earl & Beverly Hines

FLORAGOLD ruffled top comport - rare item   From the collection of Dean & Mary Watkins

The 5¼″ comports were never put into production. Approximately ten of each style (ruffled top or plain) were made. Eventually, management level employees of Jeannette ended up with the small production. A maid acquired one of each style and after selling the plain top one for $5.00, held out for $20.00 on the ruffled style. Only three of the ruffled top and a few more of the plain top comports can be accounted for now. When in Pittsburgh, remember to look for these!

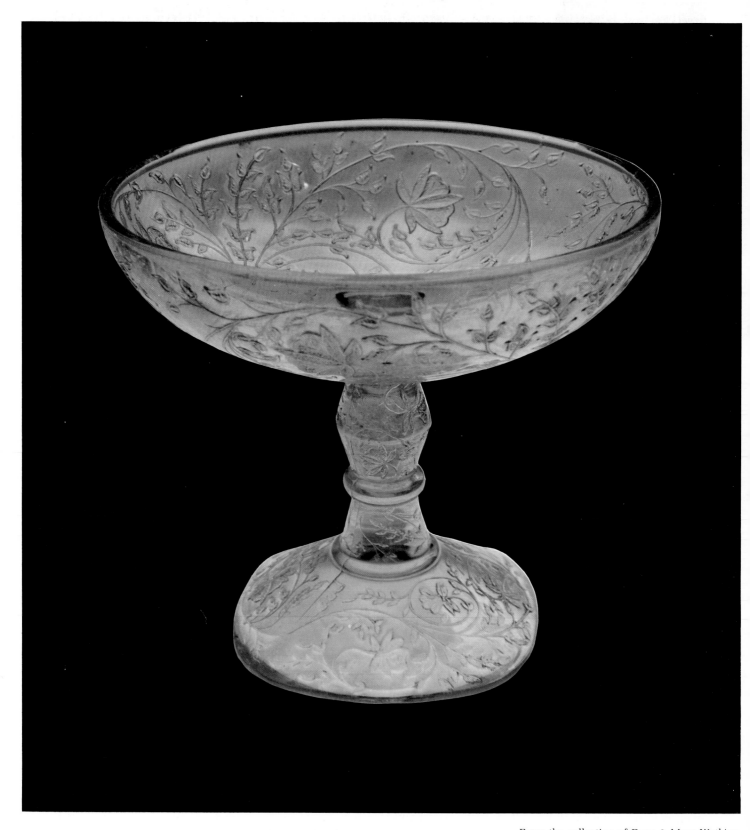

FLORAGOLD plain top comport - rare item

FLORAL green rose bowl with frog - rare items

From the collection of Earl & Beverly Hines

For years green Floral has been one of the most difficult patterns to completely garner all of the pieces available. We are beginning to understand why. Most of the harder-to-find pieces are being found in England! Some have also been found in Canada, but the ties between these two countries are quite well known. In my travels in Ontario last year, I met more than one person who was having Depression glass shipped to Canada from England. Maybe the reason that so many pieces in Floral are rare in our country is that they were not even sold or given away here. The green rose bowl is one of the pieces that has been finding its way home from England. Some of them have been coming in "container" shipments of furniture to dealers. The flower frog was purchased to fit the rose bowl and that is the only piece that it does fit. This frog has also been found in crystal, but only one frog of each color has surfaced so far.

FLORAL green comport - rare item

From the collection of Nancy Maben

Note that the green Floral comport has a ruffled edge. It is a different shade of green than the rose bowl.

FLORAL pink comport - rare item

The pink comport has a straight edge. I have not seen enough of these to know whether all green are ruffled and all pink are straight—so if you have one that has the opposite edge, let me know.

FLORAL pink cream soup - rare item

Author's collection

The Floral cream soup is difficult to find in either color. It is unlike any other cream soup in any other pattern except Doric. Both of these patterns have cream soups that look as if they have had handles applied to a regular bowl. It's more like an afterthought than good planning. Maybe glass design persons did not yet have a feel for what was wanted by the public. In any case, FEW survived for us to criticize.

WINDSOR red pitcher and tumbler - rare color

From the collection of Earl & Beverly Hines

Windsor in red (actually, amberina) would make a great set. You will have to settle for maybe a piece or two. Only a few of the red pitchers and tumblers have appeared. Red color is obtained by placing glass back into the furnace to reheat it. It is yellowish when placed back inside. If the reheating is not evenly done, then there are yellowish tints that show. Hence, the term amberina is used to describe this reddish-yellow color.

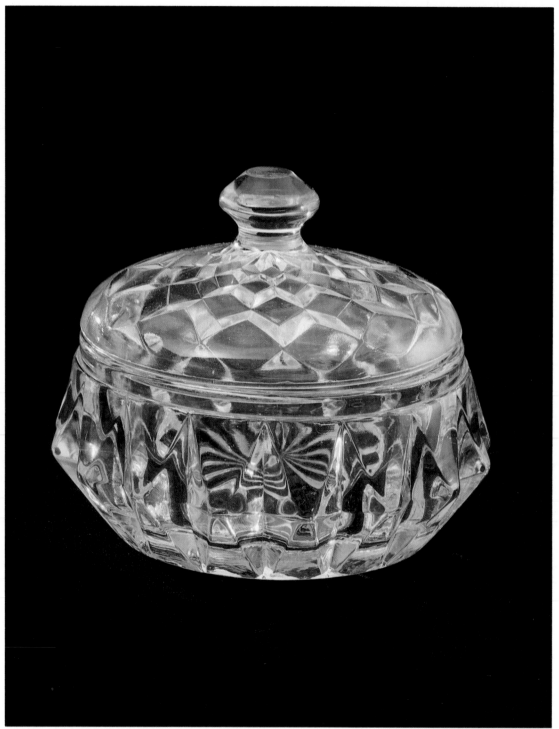

Author's collection

WINDSOR yellow powder jar - rare color

This is the only known piece of canary yellow or vaseline in this pattern. This was found along with the Cube powder jar. Note that the Windsor has a Cube top. They look interchangeable. They are not! The two powder jars are different shades of yellow and the lids will not mix because of the color variations.

MACBETH-EVANS GLASS COMPANY 1899-1937

Macbeth-Evans made some of the more popular Depression patterns, but as in other companies' wares, some pieces are in such short supply, they're deemed quite rare finds.

Pitcher from the collection of Earl & Beverly Hines   Tumbler from the collection of the Author

DOGWOOD pink pitcher and juice tumbler - rare items

The Dogwood pitcher in the "S" Pattern shape has always been hard-to-find. The reason for this seems to have been discovered. They are turning up in the Phillipines. It seems a lot of our glass went over there as promotions for Hershey's chocolate or as ship ballast. A member of our Navy brought back three pitchers but left one because it cost $25.00. Evidently, this is another item in short supply because it was sent out of the country and not because only a few were made. The juice tumbler shown beside the pitcher is even more rarely seen than the pitcher. The only time more than one or two were found at the same time was at the first National Depression Show in 1976. Since that time only a few more have surfaced.

DOGWOOD red berry bowl - rare color

A few pieces of red Dogwood have been reported over the years. It stood to reason that it was possible since the company's American Sweetheart pattern had both red and blue in its line and was being made during the same time period. I had never been able to confirm the red until the bowl shown here was mentioned to me at a show in Indianapolis. A picture was sent proving its existence and now the owner is willing for all to see. It was found at a small Flea Market for less than $10.00.

From the collection of Martha Beals

"S" PATTERN green pitcher and tumbler - rare color and decoration

The "S" Pattern pitcher and tumbler with a silk screen decoration are rarely seen. You can find a plain pitcher without the decoration quite easily. Without the pattern, however, it is neither "S" Pattern nor Dogwood—no matter what anyone says. It cannot be called anything except a plain Macbeth-Evans pitcher if it has no discernible pattern. The pitcher and tumblers in pink "S" Pattern are almost as difficult to find as the green.

McKEE GLASS COMPANY 1853-1951

Originally founded as McKee & Brothers Glass Works at Pittsburgh in 1853, this company moved to a site east of Pittsburgh in Westmoreland County in 1888 and built its new plant there. This site became the town of Jeannette. The move had been necessitated by the availability of natural gas in this area. Later, with the depletion of this natural gas, the company turned to the other readily available resource in the area—coal. McKee continued making glass at this site until 1951 when The Thatcher Glass Company bought the company.

When McKee is mentioned today, two things seem to stand out in collector's minds: Rock Crystal and kitchenware items. Collectors of Depression patterns immediately think of the red or crystal of the Rock Crystal pattern that was made from the early 1900's up until the 1940's. The kitchenware lines of reamers and measuring cups have come to the forefront of collecting in recent years. There were many other kitchenware items made, but these two categories have some of the most avidly sought items.

MEASURING CUPS - rare colors   From the collection of Terry & Celia McDuffie and Author

Most McKee measuring cups are collectible. However, the one cup, two-spouted variety is the most coveted. Color varieties as well as scarcity make this cup one the most desirable to own! The taller quart measure is as rare except in Jadite. The Seville yellow and Chalaine blue shown are the only ones known in those colors. There are more collectors for the one cup type, but do not pass by that quart measure if you see one!

REAMER ultra-marine Sunkist - rare color

From the collection of Terry & Celia McDuffee

The Sunkist line of reamers are known for their diversity of color. Reamer collectors, in particular, search for every shade and variation possible. A swirl of color, or lack of that swirl, as well as embossing or lack thereof, can mean lots of dollars made or spent. One of the latest finds is the ultra-marine colored Sunkist shown here. It was found at a show in Oregon. Many of the harder-to-find reamers are found on the West coast. Premium items which advertised the California fruit juice market make this area fertile ground for today's reamer collectors.

PADEN CITY GLASS COMPANY 1916-1951

   Paden City Glass Company built its factory and started producing glassware all within a one year time period. That was considered quite a feat in 1916. We think of Paden City as a company which produced a multitude of colors and made a variety of patterns containing birds. This handmade glass was not turned out in the large quantities that many of the glass factories of that day produced. Hence, items manufactured by Paden City are even more scarce fifty years later. Most of the glassware made by this company is exceedingly attractive in design and line.

Author's collection

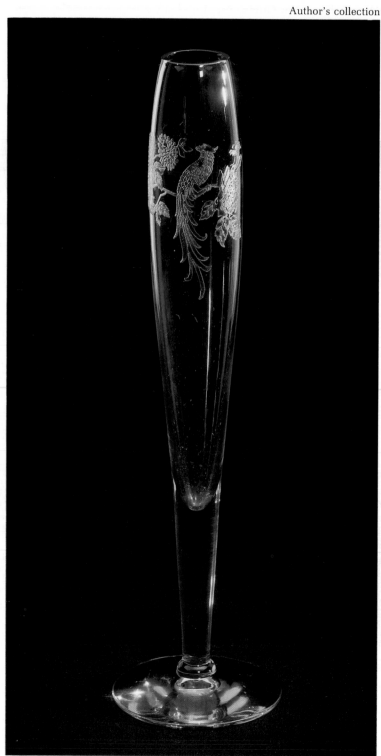

PEACOCK REVERSE pink vase - rare item

   The pink vase stands 10″ tall and is one of a very few to be seen. Pink is the only color that I have seen.

U.S. GLASS COMPANY 1891-1962

The U.S. Glass Company was founded in 1891 as a merger of eighteen smaller companies in Ohio, Pennsylvania and West Virginia. The branch known as "R" factory was located at Tiffin, Ohio, and was better known as the Tiffin Glass Factory. Flower Garden with Butterflies (or just "Flower Garden" to many collectors) is the pattern thought of when U.S. Glass is mentioned. Most pieces in this pattern are hard to find. The heart-shaped candy remains the dream of many collectors, but it does exist. My favorite piece of "Flower Garden" is the candlestick with glass candle. Even the candle has the design!

FLOWER GARDEN with BUTTERFLIES blue candy - rare item and color

The blue heart-shaped candy is one of two known. This piece is hard to find in any color!

FLOWER GARDEN with BUT-TERFLIES black candle and candlestick - rare item

The black candlestick is 6″ with a 6½″ glass candle. It is one of a pair and although shown in old catalogues, this was the first I had actually ever seen. I've since seen one other pair.

From the collection of Frank & Sherry McClain

UNKNOWN

I have included a couple of pieces that fit the Kitchenware line, but their origin of manufacture is in doubt. There is no question as to collectability; but if you have any information on them, please let me know.

MEASURE CUP peacock blue - rare color

From the collection of Nancy Maben

These are being found in the Chicago area, but so far only three or four are known. All of these were found in the latter half of 1986. Keep looking!

VACUUM THERMOS BOTTLE - rare item

From the collection of Dick & Pat Spencer

This cobalt blue piece was found in a consignment shop for $22.00 in 1986. Bottom is marked: "The American Thermos Bottle Co., Norwich, Conn. U.S.A.; Genuine Thermos Reg. U.S. Patent Office; Pat. App'd For; Vacuum Bottle". The only other I can account for is in the Cambridge Museum. It is not known why, but it always sat on Mr. Bennett's desk at the Cambridge factory.

Price Guide

Page 90
Candlewick cobalt blue sherbet - $40.00-50.00

Page 91
Candlewick crystal cut goblet - $40.00-50.00

Page 92
Candlewick crystal bowl on stem and bowl - both one of
a kind

Page 93
Candlewick crystal handle vase - $75.00-90.00
Candlewick crystal sherbet - $35.00-45.00

Page 94
Candlewick oval snack plate and cup - $100.00-125.00

Page 95
Candlewick gold inlaid on glass punch bowl -
$2,500.00-3,000.00
Candlewick gold inlaid cups - $40.00-50.00

Page 96
Candlewick green bowls - $125.00-150.00 each

Page 97
Candlewick red bowl - $125.00-150.00

Page 98
Candlewick red candlesticks - $150.00-175.00 pr.

Page 99
Candlewick slag plate - $175.00-200.00

Page 100
Candlewick slag plate - $150.00-175.00

Page 101
"Daisy", Number 620 blue plate - one of a kind

Page 102
"Pyramid", Number 610 yellow ice bucket and lid -
$500.00-550.00

Page 103
Cherry Blossom pink plate - $150.00-200.00

Page 104
Cube canary yellow powder jar - $100.00-125.00

Page 105
Doric delphite pitcher - $400.00-450.00

Page 106
Doric yellow pitcher - $750.00-850.00

Page 107
Floragold comport, ruffled top - $600.00-650.00

Page 108
Floragold comport, plain top - $500.00-550.00

Page 109
Floral green rose bowl - $400.00-425.00
Frog - $400.00-450.00
Page 110
Floral green comport - $600.00-650.00

Page 111
Floral pink comport - $500.00-550.00

Page 112
Floral pink cream soup - $500.00-600.00

Page 113
Windsor red pitcher - $300.00-350.00
Windsor red tumbler - $40.00-50.00

Page 114
Windsor yellow powder jar - $90.00-100.00

Page 115
Dogwood pink pitcher - $400.00-450.00
Dogwood pink tumbler - $195.00-225.00

Page 116
Dogwood red berry bowl - one of a kind

Page 117
"S" Pattern green pitcher - $400.00-450.00
"S" Pattern green tumbler - $40.00-50.00

Page 118
Measuring Cup, Chalaine blue, small - $450.00-500.00
Measuring Cup, Chalaine blue, tall - $500.00-550.00
Measuring Cup, black - $400.00-500.00
Measuring Cup, yellow - $350.00-400.00

Page 119
Reamer, Ultra-marine Sunkist - $350.00-400.00

Page 120
Peacock Reverse pink vase - $100.00-110.00

Page 121
Flower Garden with Butterflies blue candy -
$400.00-500.00

Page 122
Flower Garden with Butterflies black candle and
candlestick - $300.00-325.00

Page 123
Measure cup, peacock blue - $150.00-200.00

Page 124
Vacuum Thermos Bottle - $125.00-150.00

Schroeder's Antiques Price Guide

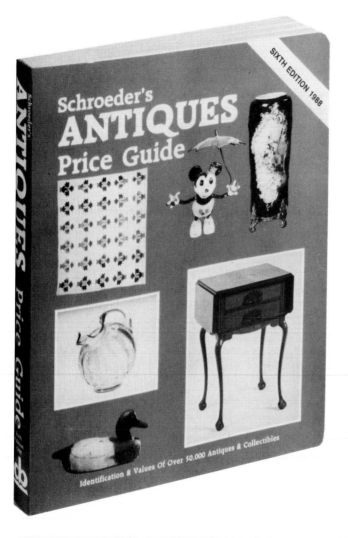

Schroeder's Antiques Price Guide has climbed its way to the top in a field already supplied with several well-established publications! The word is out, *Schroeder's Price Guide* is the best buy at any price. Over 500 categories are covered, with more than 50,000 listings. But it's not volume alone that makes Schroeder's the unique guide it is recognized to be. From ABC Plates to Zsolnay, if it merits the interest of today's collector, you'll find it in Schroeder's. Each subject is represented with histories and background information. In addition, hundreds of sharp original photos are used each year to illustrate not only the rare and the unusual, but the everyday "fun-type" collectibles as well -- not postage stamp pictures, but large close-up shots that show important details clearly.

Each edition is completely re-typeset from all new sources. We have not and will not simply change prices in each new edition. All new copy and all new illustrations make Schroeder's THE price guide on antiques and collectibles.

The writing and researching team behind this giant is proportionately large. It is backed by a staff of more than seventy of Collector Books' finest authors, as well as a board of advisors made up of well-known antique authorities and the country's top dealers, all specialists in their fields. Accuracy is their primary aim. Prices are gathered over the entire year previous to publication, from ads and personal contacts. Then each category is thoroughly checked to spot inconsistencies, listings that may not be entirely reflective of actual market dealings, and lines too vague to be of merit.

Only the best of the lot remains for publication. You'll find *Schroeder's Antiques Price Guide* the one to buy for factual information and quality.

No dealer, collector or investor can afford not to own this book. It is available from your favorite bookseller or antiques dealer at the low price of $11.95. If you are unable to find this price guide in your area, it's available from Collector Books, P. O. Box 3009, Paducah, KY 42001 at $11.95 plus $1.00 for postage and handling.

8½ x 11, 608 Pages $11.95

COLLECTOR BOOKS
A Division of Schroeder Publishing Co., Inc.